"Donna Said"

An Illustrated Self Help Journey

By

Donna Reid

TDUB PUBLISHING

HARRISBURG, PA

FOREWARD

Basic Instructions Before Leaving Earth is an acronym for the Bible. As I thought about it, I realized that basic instructions for managing our lives from an emotional, mental, and spiritual perspective would be another valuable tool.

This book is a self-help journey of thoughts and practices to manage our lives in a manner that would bring more joy, self-worth, and love into our existence. The ideas presented are taken directly from therapeutic clients embracing concepts learned through their therapy experiences. They often found that what they discovered through these personal discussions around growth and change was basic information they felt compelled to share with others.

When reporting what they told others, it appeared they were sharing these thoughts in various environments, at work, at dinner, working out, and several other lived encounters. Their messages were what Donna said and whatever thought they felt might benefit the listener.

This prompted "Donna Said," an illustrated cliff note style handbook with various seeds of thought one could apply to many situations we are presented with while being human.

Dedication

This book is inspired by and dedicated to my clients' past, current, and future. Because of you sharing with me thoughts discussed in your sessions with various people in your life, it occurred to me that it might be helpful if there was a source of quick but brief reminders of these messages you felt were critical enough to your growth to want to share them with others.

You know I cannot acknowledge you by name but know I have heard your concern for others by telling them to get " a Donna." This represents your value of the opportunity to talk out loud about some of your most private and personal thoughts and experiences.

I know I have said this to many of you, but to those who don't know me, therapy grows all parties involved, therapist and client. Speaking your thoughts out loud and having a chance to look at them from other perspectives opens your mind in an empowering way.

These "Donna Said" pieces come directly from my clients based on thoughts they felt were important enough to share with an audience like you. The different illustrations are scenes in which they have conveyed reflections.

Who is Donna?

Donna Reid, a native of Charlotte, NC, and raised in Washington, DC, is a successful self-help and counseling expert. As a licensed professional counselor Donna guides others to broaden their perspectives.

After 40 years in The District of Columbia Public School system, she retired to focus on her thriving practice, Love First, PLLC emphasizing love as life's core value.

Donna's mission is to help individuals cultivate self-love, retrain their minds, and navigate life's challenges positively. Her book, "Donna Said: An Illustrated Self-help Journey," presents transformative insights from therapeutic experiences, offering practical thoughts for diverse life situations.

Donna Reid is not just an author; she's a respected counselor inviting readers on a journey toward self-discovery and empowerment.

POSITIVENESS

If you realized how
powerful your
thoughts were,
you would never think a
negative thought

- unknown

Donna Said

We listen defensively always ready to
defend or protect ourselves from being
disrespected.

It is important to listen to learn and not to react, we often feel we must constantly watch to see if someone is disrespecting, undermining, or disregarding our voice. This style of listening often doesn't allow you to hear what the other person is saying.

LOVE

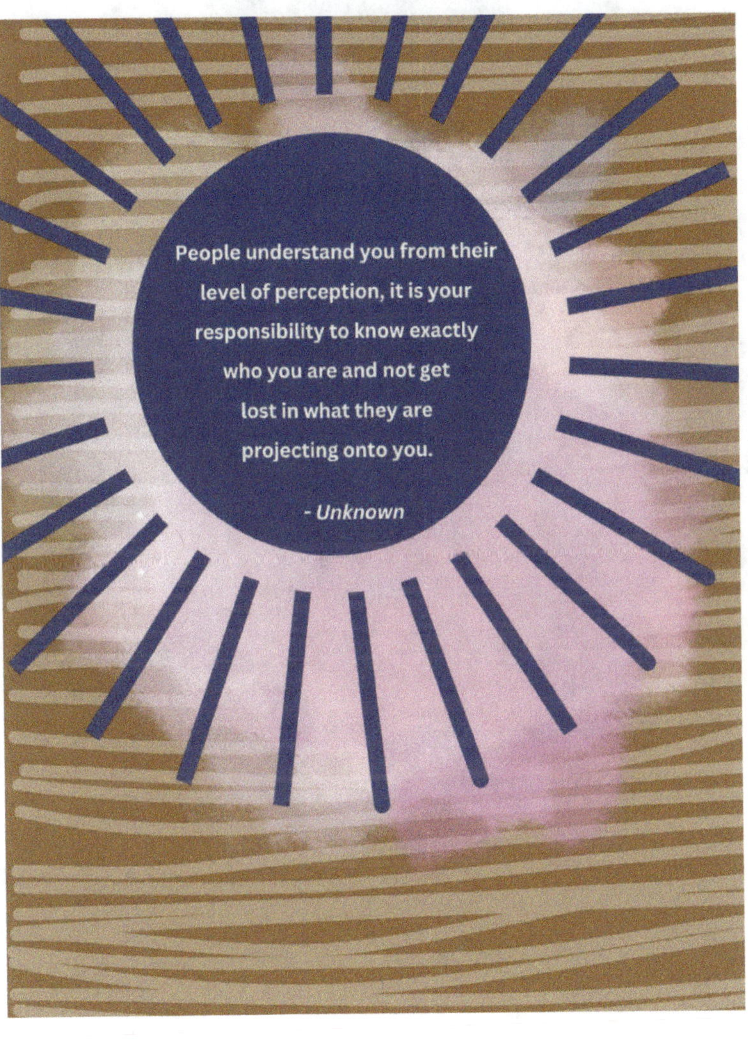
People understand you from their level of perception, it is your responsibility to know exactly who you are and not get lost in what they are projecting onto you.
- Unknown

I can choose to be happy because I'm okay.

We are responsible for our own happiness or any feelings we have. Why not choose to be okay, just like we choose easily not to be, which one feels the best?

GROWTH

Plant the seed
and watch your flower
BLOOM
-unknown

Forgiveness is for you not the other person.

When you are holding anger, grudges or disdain toward someone or self you're storing these emotions in your body and creating negative energy. No one is perfect.

Sometimes decisions and choices will be made that you may not agree with. Forgiving them frees you up and helps you to move on in a more positive way.

David Schell states, *"Sometimes people hurt you because, like you, they are learning and growing. Forgive their incompleteness, their humanness."*

BEST

MAYBE WE HEAL WHEN WE ACCEPT THAT

ITS OK TO NEVER GO BACK;

WHEN WE STOP TRYING TO USE

THE BROKEN PIECES TO REBUILD

THE OLD PICTURE AND

INSTEAD CREATE A NEW ONE

-DANIELL KOEPKE

Love yourself the best.

Loving yourself is the first step in having a loving relationship, it allows you to know your value and not depend on someone else's validation of you.

When we rely on external validation, we put too much stock in allowing others to determine our self-worth, we must love who we are just the way we are, while continuing to grow ourselves.

According to Louise Hay, *"Before you can think of working on any other relationship, you first need to focus on the one you have with yourself. Why would anyone want to be with you if you don't want to be with you."*

Life is meant to be fulfilling and enjoyable.

******

According to Louise Hay, *"your mind
is a tool to use in any way you wish.
The way you use it is only a habit,
and habits can be changed if you
want to do so. Do not think your
mind is not in your control. YOU are
in control of your mind. You can
stop thinking those old thoughts.
The thoughts you choose to think
create the experiences you have."*

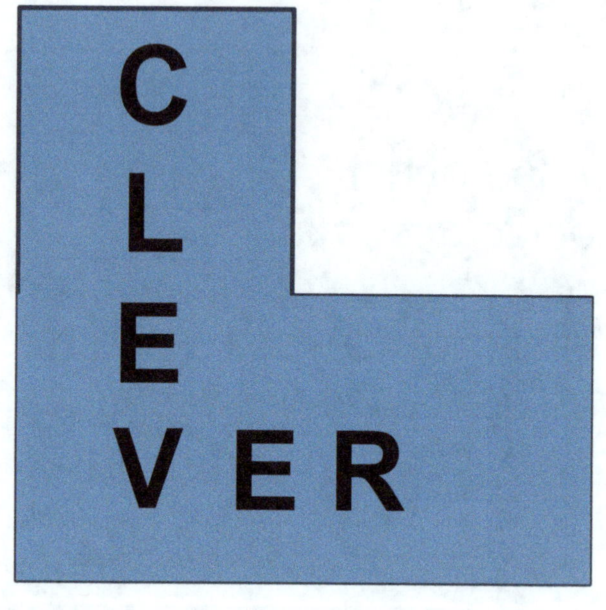

C
L
E
VER

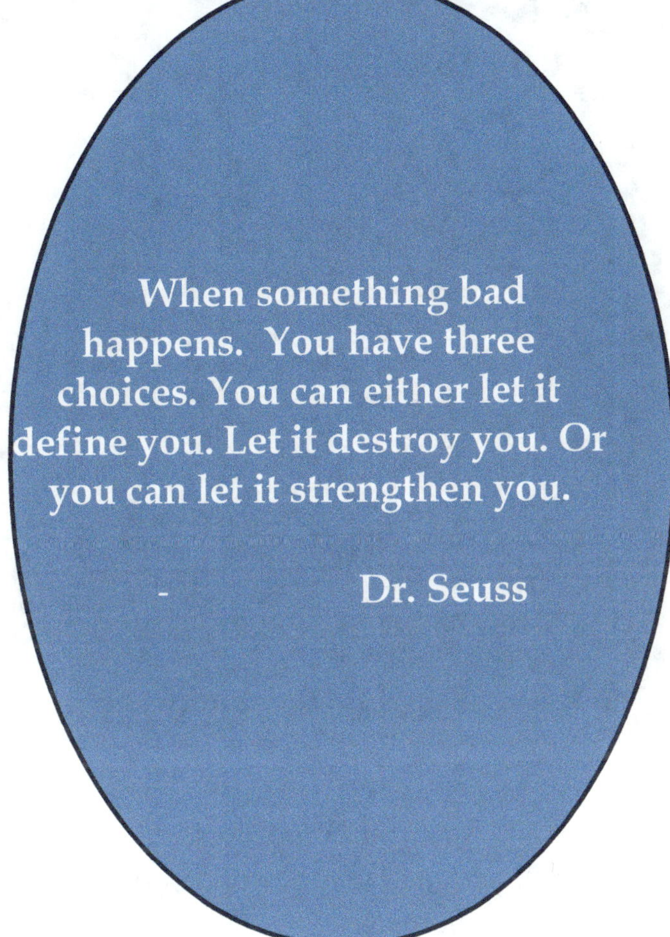
When something bad
happens. You have three
choices. You can either let it
define you. Let it destroy you. Or
you can let it strengthen you.

-                    Dr. Seuss

Communication is key to knowing each other and learning to accept and appreciate our differences.

Communicate in a way that
allows the person's perception to
be valued whether you agree
with it or not.

Hearing another persons point
of view grows your scope of
understanding information from
a variety of perspectives.

WORTHINESS

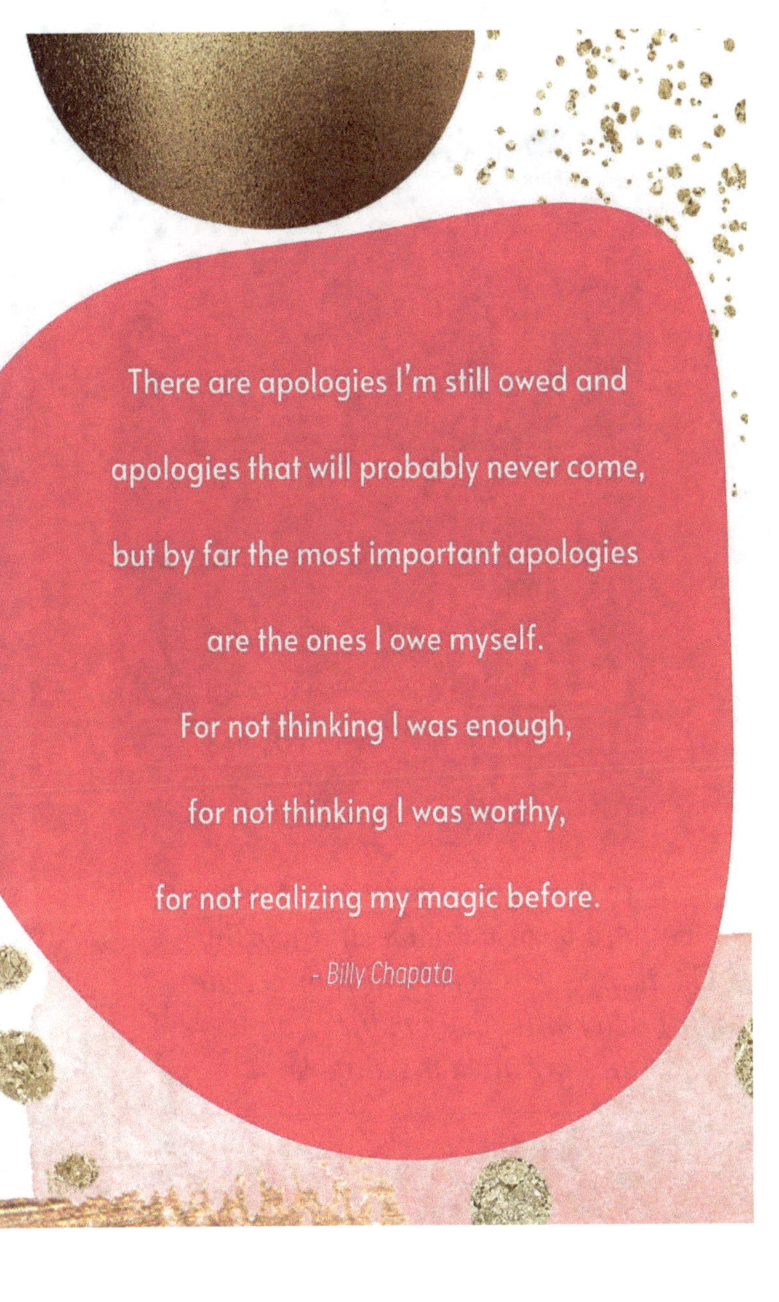

There are apologies I'm still owed and

apologies that will probably never come,

but by far the most important apologies

are the ones I owe myself.

For not thinking I was enough,

for not thinking I was worthy,

for not realizing my magic before.

- Billy Chapata

You are born valuable and worthy.
The things you accomplish or accrue
don't determine your value. You were
and are always valuable.

We are all born worthy, as we grow
messages received from people in
our lives become how we view
ourselves, unfortunately this is
directly connected to these people's
style and the positiveness with
which they critique your growth.

KINDNESS

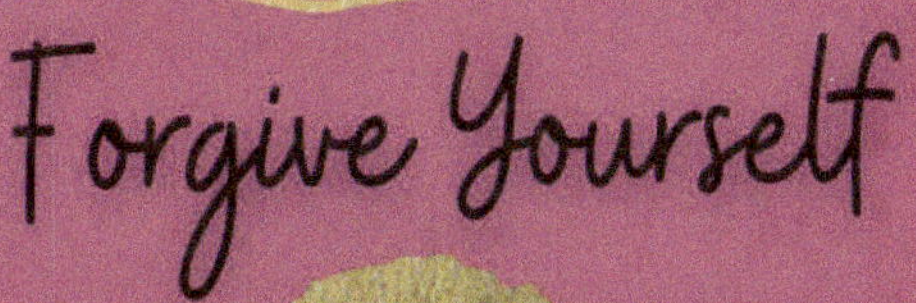

And stop dwelling on everything you think you
could have done better. The past is behind you,
and it can only control you if you let it.
So let go of what you should have
done and focus on doing the
best you can going forward.

-UNKNOWN

Donna Said

Don't let someone else's behaviors' take you out of character.

f you don't like someone's behavior toward you why present the same behavior back, this is being someone you don't like.
Don't make other people's stuff your stuff.

Og Mandino states, *"never permit anyone or anything to rain on your parade."*

"No one can ever distract you from being happy and doing your best . . . unless you give them permission to do so. Remember he who can suppress a moment's anger may prevent a day of sorrow."

SURVIVALIST

Im happy, hurting, and healing
at the same time.
Don't ask me how I'm doing it
because I don't know,
but I'm doing it and I'm so proud of myself.
-UNKNOWN

Donna Said
There is no such thing as
"I'm trying."

Choose to do, even if your task isn't complete or doesn't turn out the way you hoped, you are still doing it.

Try is a backdoor word that doesn't give the commitment you want to give your choices and can easily become "I tried" and a reason to give up.

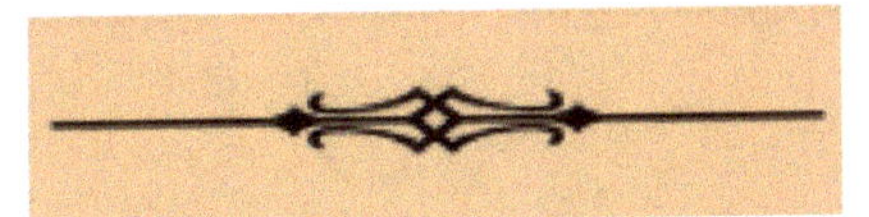

ACCEPTANCE

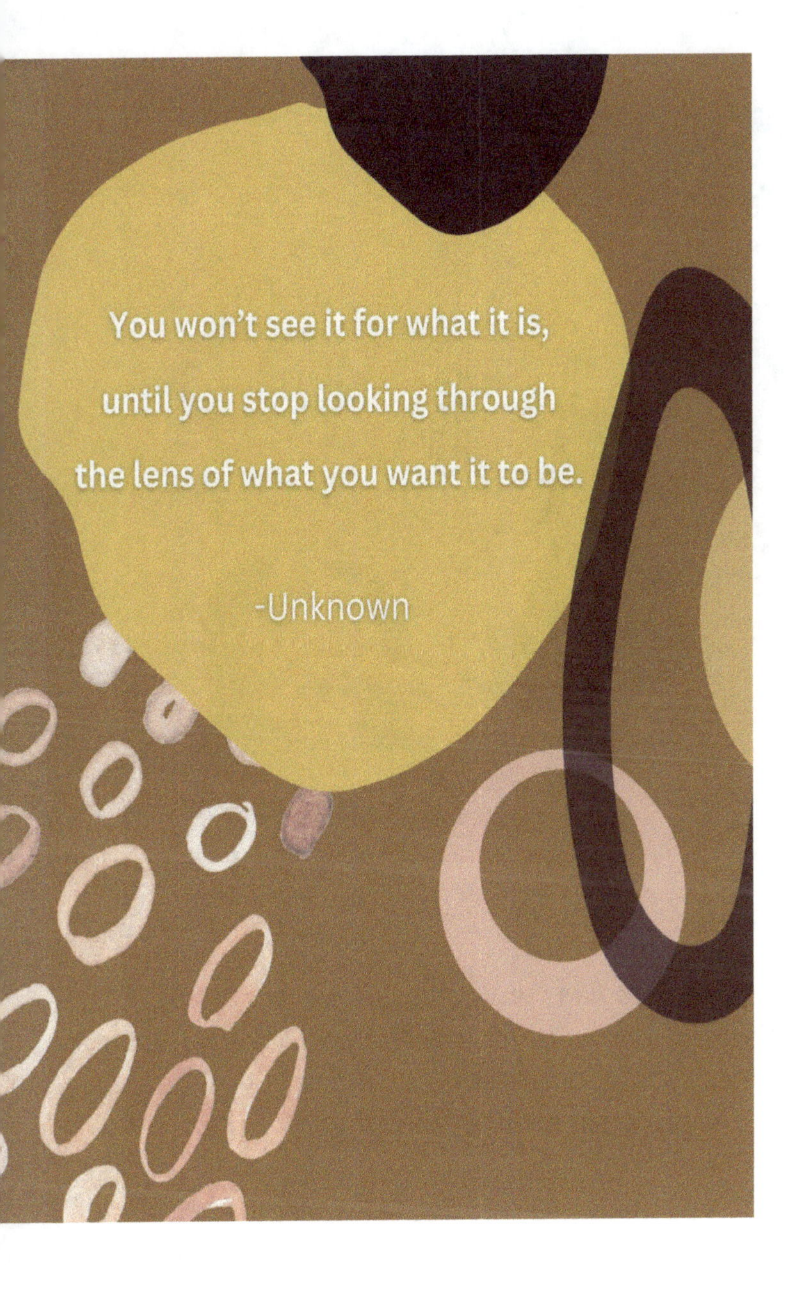

You won't see it for what it is,
until you stop looking through
the lens of what you want it to be.

-Unknown

Therapy is like having your own personal cheerleader. Life is hard and it will knock you down. Sometimes you forget how valuable you are. Therapy will remind you of your value.

You remember the bad times
more than the good times,
Because when you're struggling
you cry for a week
when you succeed you celebrate for a day.
Appreciate your wins more.

-Jay Shetty

Donna Said
You have to
Be the cake

Self-validation is an important tool for creating self-confidence. Relying on others to validate you can contribute to disappointment about self and make us question our worth. Who knows us better than we know ourselves?

We can be proud of ourselves even when no one else expresses observational pride. We are the whole cake and others are the icing, which isn't always necessary to have a good cake experience.

FORGIVENESS

Holding a grudge does
not make you strong.
It makes you bitter.
Forgiving doesn't
make you weak;
It sets you free.
-unknown

Donna Said

You cannot see or control the future; you must stay in the moment, watch situations unfold and choose your reaction.

This involves letting go of the need to control things, being observational and responsive without the Should Be's clouding your view of what is.

COURAGEOUS

When people hurt you
over and over,
think of them as sandpaper.
They may scratch and hurt
a bit, but in the end,
you end up polished and
they end up useless.

-unknown

**Throw away
negative words.**

According to Leo Buscaglia, *"words are supposed to free us, supposed to make us able to communicate, but words become boxes and bags in which we become trapped."*

Words have power. You have taught your brain a reaction to certain words, since you can't unlearn the reaction, choose words that don't cause those feelings. Imagine you keep telling yourself I'm stressing over and over what can you possibly feel but stress. The way you talk to and about yourself creates your reality.

WINNER

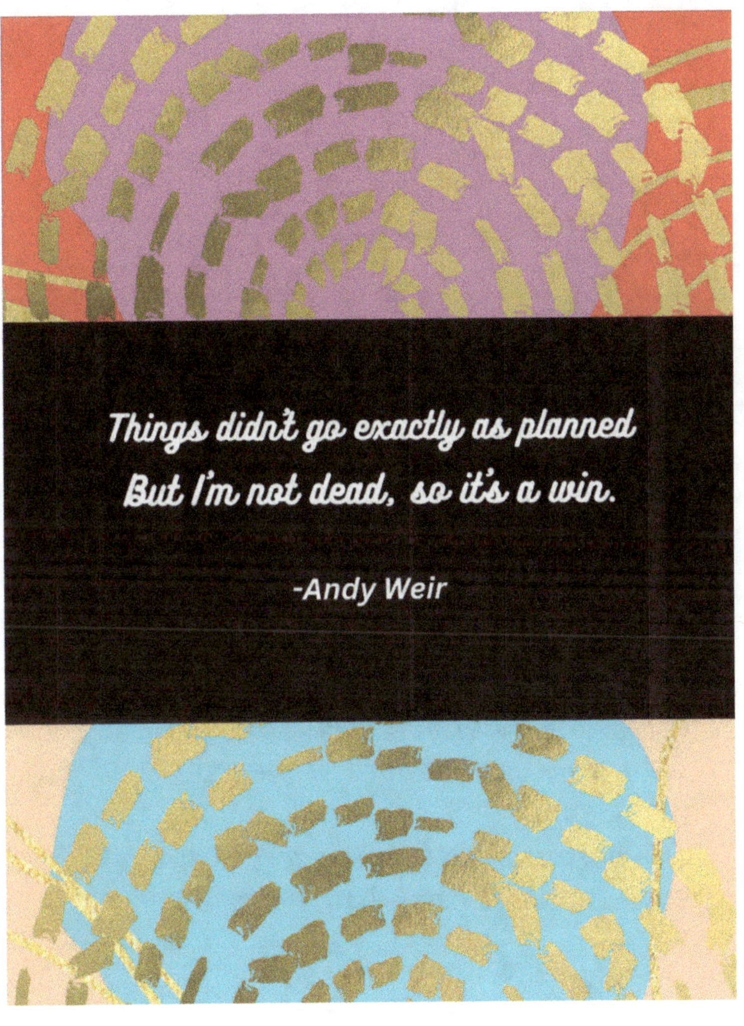

Things didn't go exactly as planned
But I'm not dead, so it's a win.

-Andy Weir

Think About it!

The possibility of you becoming your parent as you sit here in therapy because you don't want to become your parent pretty much zeroes out the possibility.

According to Harold Kushner, *"we will make mistakes…get some important things wrong from time to time. Anyone who takes the moral demands of human life seriously will make his or her share of mistakes,"* just as our parents did. Our own growth and experiences prepare us for changes in our belief systems.

NOBODY IS PERFECT

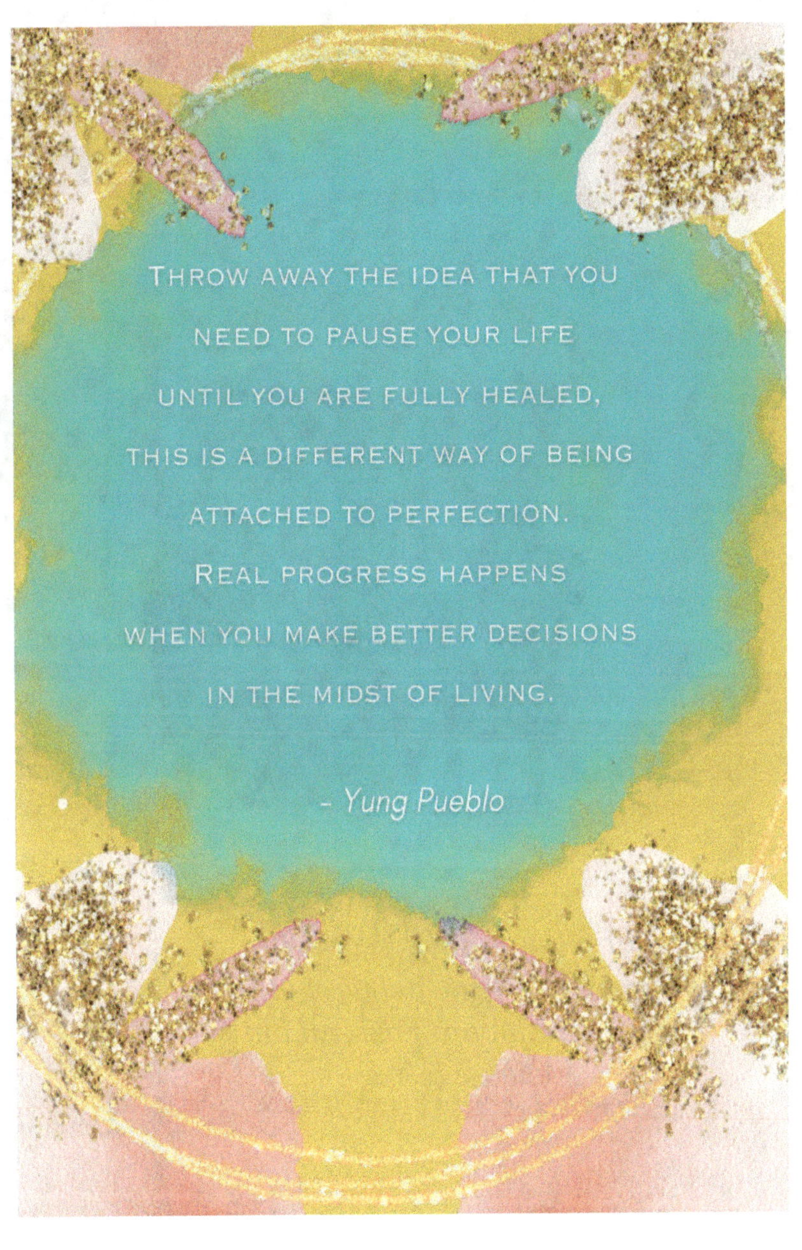

THROW AWAY THE IDEA THAT YOU
NEED TO PAUSE YOUR LIFE
UNTIL YOU ARE FULLY HEALED,
THIS IS A DIFFERENT WAY OF BEING
ATTACHED TO PERFECTION.
REAL PROGRESS HAPPENS
WHEN YOU MAKE BETTER DECISIONS
IN THE MIDST OF LIVING.

- Yung Pueblo

---

*That's their stuff. People are
different. We can't choose other
people's behaviors; we can only
choose ours.*

Often, we allow someone else's behavior to dictate how we respond and see ourselves, as opposed to seeing that we are observing their thought processes based on how they see the world.

The 2nd agreement in M. Ruiz's, The Four Agreements, *"Don't Take Anything Personally,"* states *"you take it personally because you agree with whatever was said… Nothing other people do is because of you. It is because of themselves. Even when a situation seems so personal, even if others insult you directly, it has nothing to do with you."* This is how this person sees the world. They are dealing with their feelings, beliefs, and opinions.

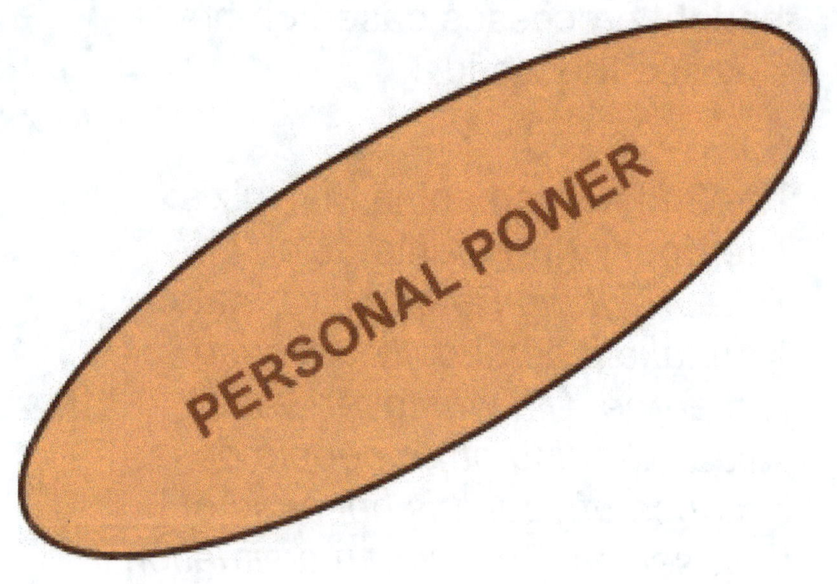

PERSONAL POWER

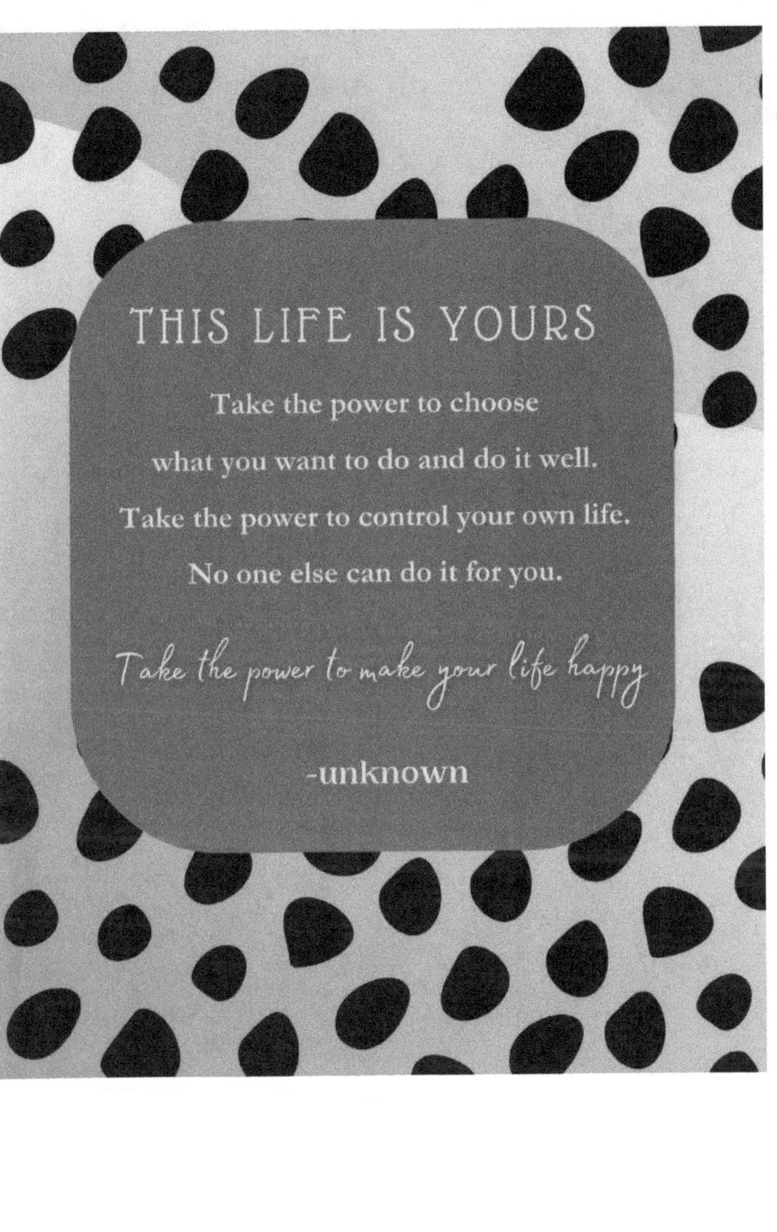

THIS LIFE IS YOURS

Take the power to choose

what you want to do and do it well.

Take the power to control your own life.

No one else can do it for you.

Take the power to make your life happy

-unknown

It's important to our growth to accept people for who they are.

We must accept that people are showing up as they currently know how to.

Unconditional love is accepting anyone you decide to interact with for who they are, not constantly finding fault and thinking it's your job to fix them.

We can expose each other to new ideas and accept that all the ideas will not be what a person will choose to do.

SELF LOVE

HAPPINESS IS WHEN YOU FEEL

GOOD ABOUT YOURSELF WITHOUT

FEELING THE NEED FOR ANYONE

ELSE'S APPROVAL

-UNKNOWN

You're always doing your best, being your best in the moment.

Your best is very fluid, and changes based on a variety of stimuli, the amount of information you currently know about something, how you're feeling that day, or your ability to grasp in the moment a concept that is being introduced.

You are doing your best because that is your personal goal/standard to do your best. Your best looks more than one way.

CONTENTMENT

Worries and tensions are like birds,

we cannot stop them from flying near us,

but we can certainly stop them

from making a nest in our mind.

- Rishika Jain

Why do you react when nothing has happened yet?

All this anticipatory fear cripples our ability to enjoy our lives. Worrying about what will happen in the future can keep us from enjoying the moment we're in.

All that is real is the moment you are experiencing, the past is just that, gone and the future is not here yet.

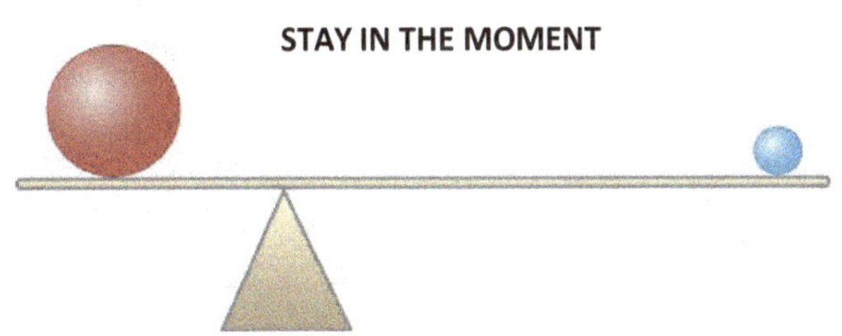

Donna Said

Worrying is a waste of time.
What does it fix ?

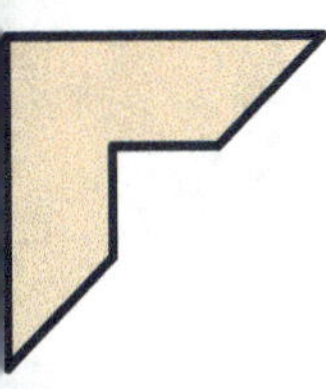

In lieu of worrying about something, why don't you think about things and decide which items you have an action for.

If there is no action take it out of your head allowing yourself not to carry things around, you can't do anything about.

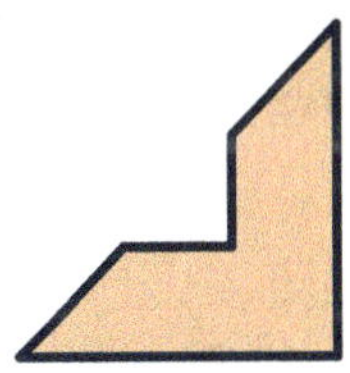

Donna Said

Be kind to Yourself

People often think that beating themselves up verbally, mentally, and emotionally is what they deserve for not being perfect.

According to Kushner, Carl Rogers states *"I am enough, not perfect. No one is perfect. Perfect wouldn't be enough.*
But that I am human, and that is enough." We are all human and will make choices that we don't like but remember that is how you learn what you do like and what works for you, it doesn't have to please others.

The idea that we are not deserving may come from our early childhood experiences, maybe we are buying into someone else's concept or opinion of us. We must create our own reality. Loving yourself is the key to this happiness we all crave.

Donna Said

"

NOT EVERYONE SHARES
THE SAME PERSPECTIVE
AS YOU. WHAT YOU VIEW
AS "RIGHT", "JUST" OR
"APPROPRIATE IS NOT
THE SAME FOR ALL.

All humans are uniquely different, and their differences create their individual value.

Accepting differences is key to having healthy and collaborative relationships, your way is not the only way to see a situation.

Opening yourself up to hearing and accepting that person's point of view validates their right to be them.

You get to maintain your belief system with the understanding that we see it differently.

DONNA SAID

"THINGS ARE TEMPORARY,
SO FIGURE OUT HOW TO MOVE
THROUGH HARD TIMES."

Don't give your personal power to what often is a fleeting situation, feel it in the moment but actively put it away, let it go and accept that this is life presenting itself with its kaleidoscope of experiences.

Don Ruiz says, *"The human is the only animal on earth that pays a thousand times for the same mistake. We have a powerful memory. We make a mistake, we judge ourselves, we find ourselves guilty, and we punish ourselves… But every time we remember, we judge ourselves again, and we are guilty again, and we punish ourselves again, and again and again."*

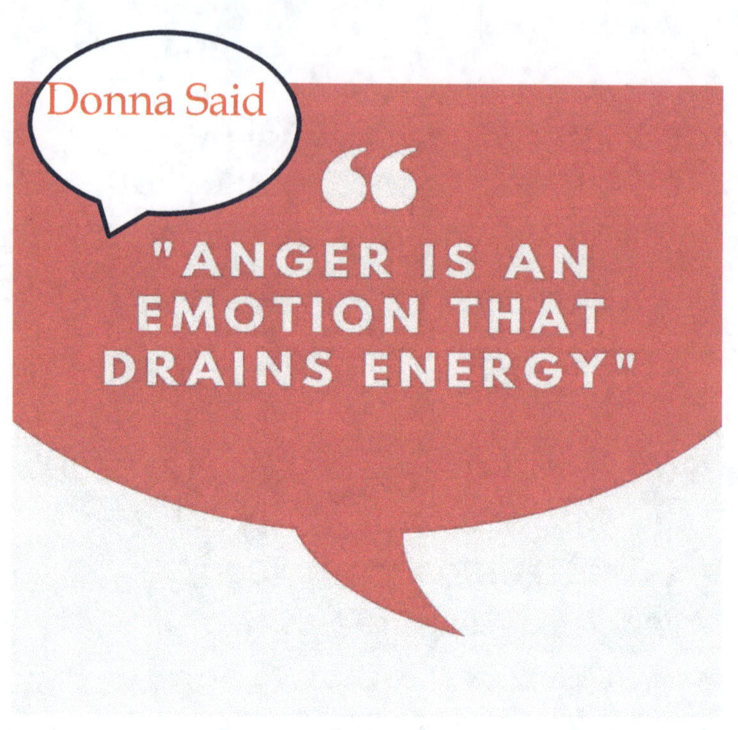

Anger is an intense emotional feeling that has many physical and mental consequences for the angry person. It can impair one's ability to be objective, empathetic and thoughtful.

Be mindful that anger doesn't correct but instead can exacerbate a situation. Your physical health is a good reminder of the importance of stepping out of a feeling and seeing it from other perspectives.

According to Louise Hay, *"Anger is an honest emotion. When it's not expressed or processed outwardly, it will be processed inwardly, in the body, and tends to develop into a disease or dysfunction of some sort."*

She further states, *"One of the best ways to deal with anger is openly talking to the person with whom you are angry and releasing the pent-up emotions."*

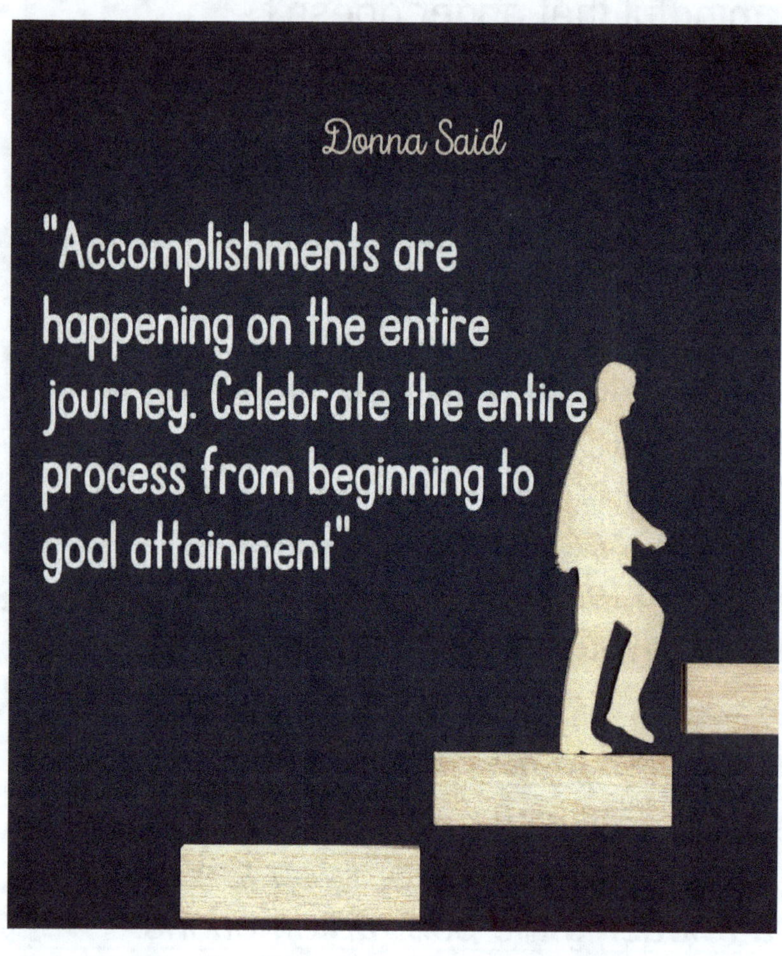

Mistakes are your stepping-stones.
L. Hay

According to Louise Hay, *"Most of us suffer from the expectation of immediate gratification. … We don't have the patience to wait for anything. We want the answers without learning the lesson or doing the steps that are necessary, but impatience is a resistance to learning."*

It is okay to make mistakes while we are learning. Anything you are going to learn takes time.

———⟨✧⟩———

PATIENCE

"Your mind will answer
most questions if you learn
to relax and wait for the
answer."
-unknown

Step away from the idea of people pleasing, decide if you like someone instead of worrying about if people like you.

People pleasing is learned behavior and how we often created relationships as we grew, making sure our parents, educators, and others were pleased by us and consequently would like us.

Building positive relationships is important but not more important than liking yourself and doing what makes your life full and satisfying.

The goal of human development is to know oneself and to live a purpose, your purpose, filled life. Everyone does not have to like you, like you don't like everyone you meet.

Awareness is the first step toward change.

Change is an important part of growth but won't be accomplished without assessing if your current outlook/behavior is meeting your needs. In other words, do I need to change something about me?

Recognize that our habits that need review often do not present directly on the surface. They are hidden in old behaviors or actions which create the delay in replacing who we are being with who we want to be.

In order to change this, we must become aware of what we need to think and do differently and then repetitiously do it. The resistance we feel makes us uncomfortable, even angry; this reaction is good as it is the first step in the change process.

Donna Said
"Not all
relationships
are for you
and it is ok
for them to
end."

Having a relationship helps you to learn information about a person and through that process you can determine if you are moving in the same way.

Change is inevitable and people moving on is not a reflection of who you are and certainly not your failure.

People enter our lives and us theirs for a reason or a season.

Donna Said

Reminder

"You are the most important person in your life, this is not vanity but matches your desire to be there for others by taking care of self."

Donna Said

"Although sad is a normal
human emotion the goal is to
not get stuck there."

Donna Said

Slow down all of that thinking. Find an abstract picture that you find beautiful. Periodically, study the picture noticing the blend of colors and the lines until all you are thinking of is the picture. This allows your brain to clear and put all those thoughts in order creating a peacefulness that is relaxing.

BEGIN YOUR JOURNEY

Reflections

Self-help books are plentiful but often difficult to navigate. After sharing with my clients' tips for managing their lives we agreed a cliff note version of these tools that you can readily have at your disposal would be valuable, this discussion prompted "Donna Said".

As I mentioned in my dedication clients were given the opportunity to be a part of this publication by sending their "Donna isims" (their term not mine).

One client, who I would be cheating if I didn't include the work he did, said the following:

Things I Learned from Donna:

"Throw the word STRESS away"—Language is so important when it comes to how we think about ourselves and the world around us and can even shape our destiny if we let it. When we use words, we start subconsciously painting a picture of the world around us and then we start to inhabit and therefore it is important to use words wisely and carefully to help shape the future that we WANT rather than the one that we have become accustomed to due to our upbringing, our childhoods and even more simply repetition.

"Don't take anything Personally" Donna borrowed this from the book "The Four Agreements" and what

this means is that we tend to be the hero (or villain) but the main protagonist in our own narrative and journey. The problem is everyone else has themselves as their own protagonist as well!
Oftentimes, we take what others do to us as a reflection of something about ourselves when it's really about how others view themselves and their lives and is a projection of their own insecurities/beliefs/reality onto us. The minute you can stop taking things personal ("nothing is personal") you can begin to step back and reflect objectively on a situation rather than reactively to any situation.

"Some people learn by bumping into things" –Donna understood that I took great care and wanted to protect my younger siblings. As a child I was parentified and I wanted to spare my siblings from the sorts of abuse and neglect that I experienced.
Fast forward into our adult years, and I tend to still be the "rescuer" in their lives, sometimes they ask for it and sometimes they don't. Donna says you can inadvertently enable people if you don't allow them to fail, and that they will never learn unless they "bump into things". Some people even need to hit "rock bottom" before they learn and people ultimately need to learn for themselves. Setting up too many safety nets can actually prevent them from learning to survive on their own. "You learned from negative experiences, didn't you?" Donna said.

Acknowledgements

We are pleased to acknowledge permission to reprint brief quotations from the following works.

Leo Buscaglia, Living, Loving & Learning. New York: Ballantine Books, 1982

Louise Hay, How To Love Yourself, A Guided Journal for Discovering Your Inner
Strength and Beauty. New York: Hay House, Inc., 2023

Louis Hay, You Can Heal Your Life. New York: Hay House, Inc., 1984

Harold S Kushner, How Good Do We Have to Be, A New Understanding of Guilt
and Forgiveness. New York: Bay Back Books/Little Brown and Company.,
1997

Og Mandino, A Better Way To Live. New York: Bantam Books, 1990

Don Miguel Ruiz, The Four Agreements. California: Amber-Allen Publishing, Inc.,
1997

David W Schell, Forgiveness Therapy. Indiana: Care Notes, 2020
R.W. Alley Illustrator

What's Next?

Visit www.tdubpublishing.com for more information about future releases from Donna Reid and for more information about the hardcover Collector's edition of Donna Said.

Don't forget to leave a review on Amazon sharing your thoughts about the book and tell all your friends too.